HERMANN'S HAUNTS

THE WINES & SPIRITS OF HERMANN, MISSOURI

BY HOLLY DRAGO & JILL PHILLIPS

HERMANN'S HAUNTS

Copyright ©2007

Printed in the United States of America.

First Edition.

ISBN 1-891442-46-5

Library of Congress number 200793490

Virginia Publishing Company
P.O. Box 4538
St. Louis, MO 63108
(314) 367-6612
www.STL-books.com
Please check out our Web site for other books on St. Louis history.

Cover Design by Ben Pierce
Inside Layout Design by Ben Pierce
Copy editor: Fran Levy. Proofreading: Laura Fister

TABLE OF CONTENTS

DEDICATION

This book is dedicated to "Caledonia," without whose love, inspiration, support and understanding this book would never have been possible.

INTRODUCTION

This book has been a labor of love. The authors have enjoyed researching the history of this lovely town, tasting the wines, meeting the people, and learning about how life used to be — a little simpler, but maybe a little spookier too — and writing about its fascinating folklore and abundant history. If you don't find something in this book that interests you, you must be dead!

We want to thank everyone with whom we talked for his or her graciousness and hospitality. A special thanks to Billy Grace and Briann Genteman at Hermannhof Winery; all of the members of the Held Family at Stone Hill Winery; Otto Klein — whose wine is superb; Jim Kinker — a curator of some truly fabulous artifacts; the ladies at Deutschheim State Historic Site for answering all of our questions; and the many others who so generously gave of their time and stories.

ORIGINS

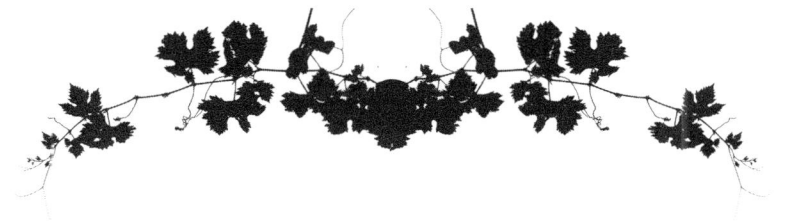

THE OSAGE INDIANS

The Osage Indians lived along the Osage and Missouri rivers in the area that is now western Missouri and were newcomers to the area, according to James Kinker, a regional historian living in Hermann. "They had come from the Pittsburgh area and were related to the Iroquois, or Eastern tribes. They came via the Ohio around 1600, and the French came down the Mississippi about the same time and found the Osage in the region. For 150 years, the Osage controlled Middle America. The French helped the Osage and sold arms to them, and the Osage in return kept out the Pawnee and Apache. Most of the Osage men were 6-1/2 to 7 feet tall." President Thomas Jefferson described them as "the most magnificent people on earth." They were a very proud and very intelligent people, according to Kinker.

Most of the men shaved their heads, leaving only a scalplock extending from the forehead to the back of the neck. The pattern of a man's scalplock indicated to which clan he belonged. Village life followed rules and customs established by a group of elders known as the "Little Old Men," according to Osage historian Miles J. Laban in his book *Wahkontah*. The Osage had as many rituals as did the Europeans who were arriving to the United States, Laban said, the most important being those for mourning the dead and preparing for war.

They were called the "children of middle waters." There were the Big Osage (upper) and Little Osage (lower). In their legend of the flood, some of their people stayed above the hill, and some stayed below the hill (which was a forested region of hills and mountains in the land the Osage first inhabited in mid-continent North America), according to Laban. The Osage believed that everything had a spirit.

When Jefferson be-
came President, he
wanted all the Indians
to be moved west of
the Mississippi, into
the Louisiana Terri-
tory, says Kinker. In
1815, after the Lewis
and Clark expedition,
treaties were made to
move the Osage even
further west. In 1825,
the Osage were moved
out of Missouri into
south Kansas; during
the move, their popu-
lation declined from

Osage Warriors

17,000, to 3,000. In 1870, they were moved once again, this
time from south Kansas to Oklahoma.

The Osage were shrewd, according to Kinker, and they bought
what is now their reservation from the Cherokee. The Cherokee
had been given the land by the government, and the Osage purchased the land with money the government had given them.
The limits of their present reservation were established by act of
Congress, July 15, 1870.

In 1904, the Daws Act mandated all Indians should act and
live in accordance with the laws and social norms of their new
European brothers. This act gave the Osage 160 acres to farm;
via allotment, 229 Osage received 160 acres each; however, the
acres were not adjacent to each other. Thus the Osage would
have to move about these different lots to farm the land. Upon

the death of the owner, an Osage could pass the allotment down to kin.

Even after the1904 Daws Act, the mineral rights still belonged to the tribe. As it happens, oil was found on their land, and for a time they were the richest tribe in the world. The government then required the Osage to have guardians (lawyers) to "help" them with their wealth. According to Kinker, each of the Osage received a $1000 allotment, and the rest somehow disappeared.

As of 1906, their land consisted of 1,470,058 acres. In addition, the tribe possessed funds in the Treasury of the United States amounting to $8,562,690, including a school fund of $119,911, the whole yielding an annual income of $428,134. Their income from pasturage leases amounted to $98,376 that same year, for total annual income therefore of approximately about $265 per capita, again making this tribe the richest in the entire United States.

Today the Osage continue to live on their reservation in Oklahoma.

HISTORY

THE GERMANS COME
TO HERMANN

The German Settlement Society of Philadelphia was founded in 1836 in the hope that a "Second Fatherland" could be established in America. Its members were appalled at the loss of German customs, culture, and language among the German émigrés and wanted to found a colony that would be a self-supporting refuge for German heritage and traditions.

Set up as a joint stock company, this prototype community was advertised throughout the eastern United States and Germany as the "German Athens of the West." Those seeking membership bought shares entitling them to lots of 40 acres each in the future town. The colony quickly attracted a variety of professionals, artisans, and laborers.

George Bayer headed a scouting committee in 1837 to the selected site on the Missouri River. A schoolmaster and musician who had emigrated in 1830 from Karlsruhe, Baden, on the Rhine River, Bayer purchased 11,300 acres of Frene Creek Valley land for $15,612 on behalf of the Society. His choice for the site, bounded by hills and bluffs on three sides and the Missouri River on the north, and teeming with wild grapes, was apparently influenced by its similarity to the Rhine River region in Germany.

The Society modeled the layout of the colony on that of Philadelphia and expected the city to become one of the largest in the United States. In their optimistic plan, they wanted to include a Market Street ten feet wider than its namesake in Philadelphia. The city was named after Hermann (Arminius in Latin), who had defeated the Roman legions in 11 A.D., claiming that this leader and his virtues embodied a symbol for their great dream.

George Bayer was appointed general manager and instructed to survey lots, act as land agent, arbitrate all disputes, establish a school, and take up the duties of schoolmaster. Unfortunately, Bayer was delayed by illness and did not arrive in Hermann until the early spring of 1838. By that time, the first small group of eager settlers, who had arrived in

mid-December 1837, were disgruntled and resentful. Their unrealistic vision of rural life in the west had been shattered by the grim reality of a harsh winter in the wilderness, during which they depended for survival on the kindness of a few hardy French residents.

Letters of complaint (many totally unfounded) regarding Bayer's management were sent to Philadelphia. The colonists were so difficult, and the tasks assigned to him so impossible, that in October of 1838 Bayer was relieved of his duties. Saddened and disillusioned, Bayer died "of a broken heart" in March of 1839. He was buried in disgrace in the most remote corner of the city cemetery he had platted, and directions were given that no one was to be buried within 75 feet of his grave.

On July 1, 1839, the 450 residents of Hermann separated themselves from the parent society in Philadelphia. Although this decision was rash, the tenacity of the early settlers and their descendants and the well-organized framework provided by the Society have allowed the town to endure and to pursue its cultural dream in spite of two World Wars, Prohibition, and the Depression.

George Bayer's grave

During Hermann's 150th anniversary celebration in 1986, a court of inquiry, after months of investigation, formally exonerated George Bayer of any wrongdoing in the management of Hermann, and today the founder finally has the recognition and honor he deserves.

Since the 1950s Hermann has encouraged a renewed interest in its unique heritage. Nowhere is the town's pride in its history more evident than in the architectural restorations throughout the village and its countryside. The dream lives on.

GERMAN RATIONALISM AND ITS HERMANN PROPONENTS

BY BRUCE KETCHUM, HISTORIC SITE ADMINISTRATOR

DEUTSCHHEIM STATE HISTORIC SITE

The foundations of the 18th century Enlightenment movement began in Europe in the 17th century with scientific inquiry, in which mathematics and empirical observation became the means of a larger understanding of the world. In France, René Descartes applied mathematical theory in his work *Discourse on Method* (1637). England's Isaac Newton explained the law of gravitation in *Mathematical Principles of Natural Philosophy* (1687) by the use of empirical observation and mathematical theory.

"Natural law" was the term used for these new approaches to understanding the world. The application of natural law was expanded by John Locke to include theories on the function of government: in *Two Treatises of Government* (1688), he suggested that when the government acts in accordance with the natural law of human beings it operates in their best interests.

France emerged as the European leader of philosophical development in the latter half of the 18th century. French philosophers such as Jean-Jacques Rousseau and François-Marie Arouet Voltaire wrote essays, books, and plays that imparted the Enlightenment beliefs throughout Europe and even to America. In the late 18th century, the philosophical tenets of Enlightenment evolved into a new movement that became known as *German Rationalism*.

By the 19th century, German philosophers began to influence the Enlightenment. Friedrich von Schiller, Johann Gottlieb Fichte, Christian Furchtegott Gellert, Johann Wolfgang von Goethe, Immanuel Kant, Friedrich Hegel, and Gotthold Ephhraim Lessing expressed advancement in the field of thought.

German universities exposed young men to a rich intellectual environment.

Eduard Muehl was a theology student at the University of Leipzig

Shed at Deutschheim State Historic Site

from 1821 through 1843. During this time, Muehl was drawn into this environment of expanding thought. Even though he had been raised the son of a conservative Lutheran minister, he embraced the new ideas to which he was exposed.

But the liberal thinking and Rationalist religious perspective that he developed in college closed the door to a permanent pastoral position when his studies ended. Denied the opportunity to serve in the clergy, Muehl left the German states in 1836 for America, where he would eventually establish a new career in journalism.

Most German Rationalists believed in a creator; however, some were agnostic and some were atheists. The philosophies of German Rationalism and English Deism, which developed at about the same time, were nearly identical. English Deism espoused a belief in one God, a Creator. Deism was the primary religious philosophy of the founders of the United States.

Deists believed that no sacred texts had been authorized by the Creator, nor had the Creator founded any religion or spoken to human beings. The natural world all around us, and the scientific principles on which its functions are based was the word of God to a Deist. Most Deists and Rationalists had studied the philosophical teachings of Je-

HERMANN'S HAUNTS

Strehly House at Deutschheim State Historic Site

sus and the Bible: The light of reason was used to question all beliefs, and blind obedience to tradition was rejected. Ancient people were thought to have believed in mysticism and miracles only because of their primitive understanding and lack of comprehension.

Mathematics, empirical observation, and the study of the developing sciences were the keys to explaining and understanding the Creator and those things previously beyond human understanding. The cornerstone of both German Rationalism and English Deism was a reliance on reason and freedom of thought. These, they thought, were God given.

German communities in Missouri, such as St. Louis and Hermann, were home to a significant number of German Rationalists. However, there were Rationalist societies in almost every area of the country with a sizable German immigrant population. In Ohio: Akron, Dayton, Toledo, Cleveland, Sandusky, Hamilton, Columbus, Cincinnati, and Massillon. In Wisconsin: Sauk City and Milwaukee. Texas was entirely founded by Rationalists.

German Rationalist societies were prominent in Illinois: Galena and Chicago; in Indiana: Evansville and Indianapolis; in Iowa: Dubuque and Davenport; in Kentucky: Louisville; in Louisiana: New Orleans;

in Maryland: Baltimore; in New York: Buffalo and New York; and in Pennsylvania: Pittsburgh.

Eduard Muehl was the inspirational leader in the Hermann area. People were motivated to think through his poetry, newspaper writings and oratory. Hermann's first newspaper, the *Licht-Freund* ("Friend of Light") was a Rationalist newspaper established by Eduard Muehl and his brother-in-law, Carl Strehly. The first edition was published in August, 1843. Through the *Licht-Freund*, Muehl and Strehly hoped to disseminate the light of the truth among their countrymen. But only a few could, or did, appreciate this paper. The strenuous struggle for an existence in this new land took up most of their time; they had little time for philosophical discourse. In consequence, the publication became unprofitable. In 1845, the *Licht-Freund* was abandoned, replaced by the *Hermanner Wochenblatt*, a paper of news in the general sense.

In 1852, Muehl founded a Rationalist group called the Union of Free Men. Strehly and a few other members of the community were also involved. With an opening poem about freedom, Eduard Muehl roused the group at their first meeting on April 4th. There were 51 charter members; Carl Strehly was named President of the organiza-

Wine Cask

tion. The group organized a modest Freethought library and formed a choir. Meetings were held in the Erholung building on Second Street. Notices for meetings of the Union of Free Men were carried by the *Hermanner Wochenblatt* newspaper.

A view of special respect was held for Deist George Washington, and in fact all the Founding Fathers were viewed as heroes by the German Rationalists. *The Age of Reason* by Revolutionary War writer Thomas Paine was also highly respected. Each year on January 29th, Rationalists celebrated Thomas Paine's birthday. They also held a celebration of spring every year, and of course they fêted Independence Day.

The source of inspiration for the Hermann-area Rationalists ended with the death of Eduard Muehl on July 7th, 1854. Hermann endured a severe cholera outbreak during June and July; Muehl and his daughter Rosa both died.

Within just a few years of his death, no record of the Union of Free Men or other Rationalist activity in the community can be found. However, for several decades after Muehl's death, Hermann was still known as a place of Freethinkers.

Rationalism also began to fade in other parts of the country in the late 19th century. The immigrant German Rationalists had aged and passed away, and an era passed with them.

In the United States today, a distinct group of German Rationalists no longer exists; however, the philosophy, and people who believe in freethinking, still exist in a variety of freethinking groups.

DANIEL BOONE

Daniel Boone

Daniel Boone was born in Pennsylvania in October, 1734. He became a popular man in folklore, even during his own lifetime. Because Pennsylvania at that time was part of the frontier, Boone got his first rifle at an early age. It was said that he killed a panther with his squirrel gun as it leapt toward him. This was just one of the stories that made him the legend that remains to this day.

During his lifetime, he moved from Philadelphia to North Carolina, West Virginia (which was then Virginia, not yet divided) Kentucky, and Missouri. On August 14, 1755, he married Rebecca Bryan, a neighbor.

Much of his time was spent hunting. He went on hunting trips for weeks and months on end. Different animals would be hunted at different times of the year — for example, deer in autumn, and otter and beaver in winter. Native Americans ate the meat in the beavers' large, flat tails. Our research into how beaver is cooked indicates that the tail is the best part; it should be boiled or seared to remove all the excess fat, and the cooking should be done outside to avoid the smell inside your house. Because of the gamy, greasy taste, some people love beaver tails and other people hate them. Since there are no references of any kind (from the past or present) about cooking or eating river otter, one can safely say they are not palatable; Boone probably hunted them for their pelts.

Taxes were going up as white settlers expanded west. As populations increased in an area, game and hunting became more scarce. Most people did not have money and used the barter system. The government agreed to trade buckskins for a dollar — one buck, one dollar.

Legend has it that Boone did not like civilized life in Kentucky. But history shows that while he was in Kentucky, he was a tavern owner, horse trader, surveyor, and land speculator. He was a better hunter than a businessman. He left Kentucky behind and moved his family to what is now West Virginia. Bad business deals and more population made Boone decide to move to Missouri, or what was known then as "Spanish Louisiana."

Boone had been awarded land grants verbally by the Spanish government. In 1804, when Missouri became part of the United States, Boone's land claims were voided, but after several years of petitioning, they were restored. He sold the land and paid off his Kentucky debts.

When Boone moved to Missouri in 1799 and the territory was known as "Spanish Louisiana," the legal requirement that all immigrants had to be Catholic was not enforced because the Spanish were eager to populate the sparsely populated region. Boone was appointed commandant (military leader) and syndic (judge and jury) of the Femme Osage district by the Spanish Governor. He served in both these posts until 1804, when the Louisiana Purchase was completed and the territory became part of the United States. At this time, Boone lost his land grants, which had been given only verbally, and had to petition Congress to restore them. Congress reconfirmed his land grants in 1814.

His final days were spent in Missouri, although, one story says that in his older years, he went on an extended hunt along the Yellowstone River. In any case, his legend does not end with his death. He was buried in his family plot next to his wife Rebecca. The graves were unmarked. Boone's legend was big, so much so that delegates from Kentucky were said to have come to the Boone home in Missouri, demanding that Boone's remains be given them to take to Kentucky, where he was to be honored. His family was strongly encouraged to disclose the site of Daniel Boone's interment. After much persuasion, his family pointed out his grave, and the delegates from Kentucky dug up and moved the remains to their state. The burial site was decorated and advertised as a Kentucky historic site.

A plaster cast of Boone's skull was made before the Kentucky reburial, and it was later announced that it might be the skull of an African American. No explanation was given as to why the anthropologist did this reasearch. Once again, the state of Missouri could claim ownership of the burial site of Daniel Boone.

1849 GOLD RUSH

In January 1848, James Wilson Marshall discovered gold while constructing a sawmill along the American River northeast of present-day Sacramento. The discovery was reported in the San Francisco newspapers in March but caused little stir because most did not believe the account.

The spark that ignited the gold rush occurred in May 1848, when Sam Brannan, a storekeeper in Sutter's Creek, brandished a bottle filled with gold dust around San Francisco shouting "Gold! Gold! Gold from American River!" The residents of the city now had proof of the discovery, and the stampede to the gold fields was on. San Francisco's harbor was soon cluttered with derelict ships deserted by their crews. Workers abandoned their jobs — San Francisco's two newspapers were forced to close their doors because their employees had been struck by gold fever. The populations of many of the coastal towns were depleted as prospectors headed to the gold fields.

The *New York Herald* printed news of the discovery in August 1848, and the rush for gold accelerated into a stampede. Gold seekers traveled overland across the mountains to California (30,000 assembled at launch points along the plains in the spring of 1849) or took the roundabout sea routes: either to Panama or around Cape Horn and then up the Pacific coast to San Francisco. A census of San Francisco (then called "Yerba Buena") in April 1847 reported that the town consisted of 79 buildings, including shanties, frame houses, and adobe buildings. By December 1849, the population had mushroomed to an estimated 100,000. The massive influx of fortune seekers Americanized the once Mexican province and ensured California's inclusion as a state in the union.

As related by *Missouri Folklore Society Journal*:

> In March of 1850 George Husmann, like many of his Hermann contemporaries, set out on the trail west. While Hussman was away panning for gold in Gold Rush of 1849, Carl Teubner, his brother-in-law and mentor, died unexpectedly in September of 1851. When the saddened adventurer returned to Hermann, in March of 1852, he assumed the duties of manager of the extensive

Teubner nursery for his widowed sister. In his absence the Hermann wine industry had continued to grow, but Hermann's wine reputation suffered quite a bit in that its winemaking now did not match its earlier reputation.

According to "The California Gold Rush, 1849" EyeWitness to History, www.eyewitnesstohistory.com (2003):

Around 1852, articles were printed that indicate while grape rot, frosts, and other natural viticultural hazards constantly threatened the harvest, an even greater threat to the grapes existed after harvest, in the cellars. Most Missouri winegrowers were not well-enough educated with standard winemaking procedures and equipment.

THE EXPLOSION OF THE
BIG HATCHIE RIVERBOAT

Accidents on the river were not infrequent in the days of the great steamers and packet boats. Sometimes the captains would race one another, because there were no regulations on the river at that time, only to have their friendly competition end in disaster. Sometimes the boats had mechanical problems that ended in injury and death. The explosion of the *Big Hatchie* on June 23, 1842, (or 1845; two different years have been quoted) was no exception.

At least 38 people were killed, most of them German immigrants bound for Kansas via St. Joseph. Many of the victims were scalded when the *Big Hatchie* burst her starboard boiler. There was a loud explosion, which could be heard far and wide. The steamer hood was forced straight forward. Steam shot out and carried the main cabin off its foundation, pushing it aft. Many injured passengers were placed on other riverboats going to St. Louis. But many had to be cared for in Hermann. The heavy midsummer workload in Hermann left no time for coffins or funeral arrangements for those who perished in the incident. The dead were buried in the Hermann cemetery in a trench, where an obelisk stands as a reminder of the tragedy. The inscription reads:

> In Memory of the early pioneers who perished in the Explosion of the Steamboat *Big Hatchie* at the wharf at Hermann in 1842. The 35 dead that lies buried here in unmarked graves and the many whose bodies were never recovered from the waters of the Missouri River. – Erected by the Brush & Pallet Club, Inc.

The *St. Louis Weekly Reveille* reported:

> It becomes our painful duty, as faithful chroniclers of passing events, to record one of the most serious disasters that has occurred upon our waters since the explosion of the steamer *Edna*. The steamer, *Big Hatchie*, Capt. Frisbee, with some 40 passengers on board, in leaving the landing at Hermann about 1 o'clock on the morning of Monday, June 23rd, 1845, on her way to St. Joseph. [The explosion] making a perfect wreck of the boat spread death and desolation among the passengers and crew.

Big Hatchie grave

HERMANN AND THE CIVIL WAR

The citizens of Hermann did not wish to fight in the war, although some were dragged into it quite against their wishes. The natives like to tell a story that goes something like this: They had one cannon and a small group of men moving it around, giving the illusion that the town had much more ordnance and ammunition than they really had. The cadre of men moved the cannon successively to several of the surrounding hills, firing it off, mainly to scare off any Confederate intruders. Locals say they only had to do this one time. Apparently the story of Hermann's armaments was passed around by word of mouth because the men never had to do this again.

Overall, the Germans in Missouri were staunch supporters of the Union cause and were quick to support the Union when Southern sympathizers in Missouri attempted to take the state to the Confederacy. They were also anti-slavery; the philosophy of the day on the frontier was that of Reason and Free Thought, which is all about individuals having God-given liberties.

One of the turning points of the Civil War happened in Missouri and brought the state into the war, although its citizens had wanted to remain neutral. The Missouri State Guard had set up Camp Jackson (named in honor of Claiborne Fox Jackson, Missouri's governor) on the land now occupied by St. Louis University's Frost Campus in midtown. The State Guard was there only to maintain a watch. Sympathizers from both sides were at this camp, but all were respectful of one another's thoughts and beliefs. Governor Jackson himself and his elite group of state legislators had Southern sympathies and wanted to see Missouri join the Confederacy.

The atmosphere remained peaceful around Camp Jackson, however, until U.S. Captain Nathaniel Lyon, dressed as a woman, walked around the camp to spy on the soldiers and to learn their intentions. Lyon and his group feared that Southern sympathizers within the camp and the lack of defense would enable Missouri militia at Camp Jackson to capture the U.S. arsenal for the Confederates. So U.S. military leaders, needing the support of some Union loyalists, supplied weapons to several groups of loyal Germans and allowed them to move into the arsenal.

Camp Jackson

On May 10, 1861, just weeks after the battle at Fort Sumter, Captain Lyon gave the command for the German Home Guard forces to march on Camp Jackson; they routed the camp by marching in from several directions. The State Guard commander, General Daniel Frost, recognized the futility of the situation and surrendered.

The Missouri militia were marched out as prisoners and removed to the arsenal. During this confusion, Lyon was kicked by a horse, and more confusion ensued as his leadership was lost. The German Home Guard was then forced to stand with their prisoners for several hours while a crowd gathered. There was a lot of hostility toward the German soldiers. Rocks were thrown, and insults shouted, such as "Damn the Dutch" and "Hurrah for Jeff Davis."

Although eyewitness accounts do not agree, someone in the crowd is said to have shouted "Fire!" The German soldiers fired several shots, and then civilians in the crowd fired more. All told, about 27 people were killed, many of them simply bystanders. Also in the crowd were William Tecumseh Sherman and his son, who narrowly missed being shot themselves. Later, Sherman led several St. Louis German troops

Nathaniel Lyon

HERMANN'S HAUNTS

in his march to Atlanta. Although at times the Missourians made fun of the Germans for their broken English and plentiful beer drinking, the German soldiers are credited with helping to keep Missouri with the Union.

In 1864, the vanguard of C.S.A. Maj. Gen. Sterling Price's army, under the leadership of C.S.A. Brig. Gen. John S. Marmaduke, marched through the valley at Hermann, stopping at the Anton Walker place (circa 1858 [Missouri Historic Sites catalogue, State Historical Society of Missouri]. Judge R.A. Breuer [of Jesse James fame] and Mrs. Breuer restored this two-story limestone house.) The army stole the bread from the oven — but missed the money hidden among the rotten apples.

Envision the camp of Gen. Marmaduke spread out over the flat valley floor of First Creek. In the "Y" of Highways 100 and J was located Trautwein's Mill, powered by the waters of First Creek. Surrounding it were immense cottonwood stumps, some 6 feet in diameter. The trees had been cut to build the mill. Marmaduke, having traveled through Hermann that day, took over the mill and its flour, and his army had a feast of biscuits — rolled out on the flat cottonwood stumps, which also served later as readymade tables. Marmaduke's army of about 300 men was followed by a large contingent of guerillas, bandits, and desperadoes. The army went out to find horses and blankets, but the rest of his followers roamed over the countryside, pillaging and taking anything they could carry that pleased their fancy at the moment. One was seen riding, holding a spinning wheel. Later it was found broken and discarded.

On the local front, as related in the *Missouri Folklore Society Journal:*

The Civil War affected many Hermann citizens personally. George Hussman and his partner joined the Union forces. They served, as did a large portion of Hermann winegrowers. When they left to serve, they vied with Cincinnati and New York State for the title of premier American wine producer.

Michael Poeschel was past the age for active military service, so he chose in 1861 to establish the winery partnership of Poeschel & Scherer with Johann Scherer that later became the Stone Hill Winery.

Captain Charles Manwaring, having recently completed a term

in the state legislature, was appointed Provost-Marshall for the Second District, with headquarters in St. Louis, in June 1863. On a visit to his wife and infant son in Hermann in May 1864, bush-whackers killed Manwaring.

Husmann left the military in 1863 and returned to his vineyards. He wrote his first English essay on viniculture that year, and in January of 1869 he began publication of *The Grape Culturist*, the first monthly journal devoted entirely to viniculture. Also in 1869, Husmann achieved recognition as the authoritative voice on American grape culture and winemaking. As of that year, there were more than 1000 acres of vineyard in and near Hermann.

PROHIBITION

Prohibition arrived in 1920 with the enactment of the 18th amendment to the U.S. Constitution, popularly known as "The Noble Experiment." However, it was this noble experiment that wielded a deathblow to the wineries in Hermann, as well as the breweries in St. Louis, according to Jack Hayney, local collector of moonshine stills in Hermann, who is known as "Whiskey Jack." Locals describe him as having white hair and a large handlebar moustache that is waxed so the ends turn up toward his nose.

Prohibition did not happen all of a sudden, according to Hayney, but it had its beginning back in the 1800s. "It came in little by little over the decades, and back in the 1870s–80s, women wanted to close the saloons so that the men were not exposed to drunkenness and vice. The men had returned from the Civil War and did not want to hear anything about this," Hayney said.

Scene from Prohibition

Scene from Prohibition

But in 1920 Congress enacted the 18th amendment and the "Porters of Prohibition" began going after the local people who had stills in their homes to give them an "alco-holiday," according to Hayney. Moonshine was called "Tiger Spit, Panther Piss, Giggle Juice and bees' knees," he said, and the Native Americans called it "Kill Devil." During that era, the girls were known as "Flappers" and guys as "Lounge Lizards," he added.

Hayney said he knew of a dairy farm in the region where there had been a "column still" in the silo. "The Feds thought it was a milking machine and so they left the farm without incident," he said. "But they came back after talking it over with their coworkers, and the ole boy served some time for it.

"People had to have secret cellars in those days, and one needed to make sure that the still was a good 10-20 feet from the trap door so even if the Feds found the door, one still had a good chance of them missing the still," Hayney said.

Hayney located and bought each of the stills that make up his collection of nearly 100. About 85 percent of them were found in Gasconade County. Hayney has had to drill holes in the stills to conform to current federal law.

"Many people were making wine in the area; only a small percentage were making it legally," according to Hayney. "Prohibition shut down the winemaking industry in Hermann and in the region. The vineyards were uprooted or burned and the so were the big wine barrels."

According to Jim Held, owner of Stone Hill Winery, there were 12 wooden wine barrels, each large enough to hold 20,000 gallons of wine, assuming town folklore is correct, and each lovingly and intricately carved in low relief with a life-size figure of one of the 12 apostles. These magnificent barrels, built as much for the sake of art as for their usefulness, once graced Stone Hill Winery's largest wine cellar.

The colossal barrels lay on their sides with the carvings facing outward between the mighty arches. Now, almost nine decades later, the "Apostles Cellar" is filled with state-of-the-art stainless steel tanks and small oak wine barrels. The "Apostles" are long gone, their memory kept alive by the recollections of old-timers and Stone Hill's efforts to pay tribute to the past. But Prohibition demanded compliance. Wineries were closed; winemaking equipment was seized and either dismantled or destroyed.

"However, there is a tale that is passed down by word of mouth that tells that these beautiful barrels were carefully dismantled, stealthily transported to the railroad depot, and secretly shipped off to Germany. No one really knows if they arrived safely though," Held said.

Hermann's wine industry failed, but there were people in other parts of this country that saw the likes of the bootleggers — those who strapped a small bottle of moonshine to their leg or pushed it down inside their boot, Hayney said. "And there was 'Rum Row,' where Joseph P. Kennedy, father of President John F. Kennedy, made much of his money from the Caribbean rum brought on boats that anchored offshore, beyond the 3-mile limit near large U.S. cities on the east coast, off-loading their cargoes onto speed boats. Also at that time, Canada began exporting Canadian whiskey," he said.

Hayney also added that the term "highball" originated in St. Louis. This was a cocktail of whiskey mixed with water and called "ball." It was served in a tall glass and so became known as a "highball."

There were also many deaths from impurities left after the distilling process, Hayney said. "If a starch-based whiskey is being distilled from grains, it must be double distilled to filter out the fusil oil. These impurities killed those who were maybe unaware of the problem or those who simply did not take the time to do this," according to Hayney. "Also, at that time the tax on a barrel was $10. Today the tax on a barrel of an alcoholic beverage is $1200."

Prohibition finally ended in 1933, but in its time innocent people suffered the loss of business or loss of life; organized crime grew considerably; the legal system became increasingly corrupt; disrespect for the law grew; and overall the consumption of alcohol increased dramatically year by year during the 13 years of Prohibition, according to Hayney.

"THE OLD BREWERY" STORY

There was a place known as the "Old Brewery" that had the reputation of being haunted, according to Anna Hesse, early Hermann historian. One could see the arched opening in the hillside where it used to be, off Route 100. Belief in the old ways and in witchcraft had not entirely passed at the time of the Civil War and before, and so farmers passing through the area with their teams who had been to Hermann made it a point not to dawdle in parts near here. They made sure that they passed through quickly and before sundown.

Many horses were reported to have shied and become unmanageable here when they presumably saw what their masters did not — a spirit or a ghost. The riders, not seeing through the veil (the separation of the material versus the spiritual world), continued on their course, peering straight ahead. Some reported seeing a blinking light in the vicinity on moonlit nights. Others reported seeing a shadowy white figure floating around the brewery and on the hillside — perhaps after spending a good deal of time at a local wine cellar in Hermann.

All of these stories seem to have developed from the supposedly true story of a transient who came to the brewery soon after it was built and asked for work. He was hired, but soon after was killed in an accident. He was buried without ceremony, next to the wall of the brewery. On moonlit nights, passersby say they see a mist or a spark of light.

THE POMMER MUMMY

The Pommer mummy was a mystery for a long time; in some ways it remains so.

Dr. Pommer was a dentist whose family was among the founders of Hermann. He and his wife were world travelers. On their visit to Egypt around the turn of the last century, they purchased a mummy as a souvenir — a common practice among tourists at the time. It was said to have had mysterious eyes that would follow one through the room in which it stood.

After the Pommers had both passed away, the mummy was put in storage in their attic, where it remained for many years. No one else ever lived in the house. Eventually, one of the Pommers' nieces, a resident of Kirkwood, Missouri, retrieved the mummy. Neighbors say that she used to display it on her front porch for Halloween. At some point, however, we lose all traces of the mummy, and for a long time no one knew what had happened to it. Recently, however, it was "discovered" in the stored collections of the St. Louis Science Center. Al Wiman, Vice President of Public Understanding at the SLSC, says that the mummy was given to the Center in 1985 by an anonymous donor. (Sources at the Deutschheim House in Hermann believe the donor to have been a descendant of the Pommers.) Science Center officials recently tried but failed to locate the donor or his family.

At the request of his friend Wiman, Charles Hildebolt, a dentist and anthropologist, brought several Washington University radiologists and geneticists to study the mummy. Salima Ikram, a professor at the American University in Cairo and one of the world's foremost mummy specialists, and Florida State University anthropologist Dean Falk signed on to help.

The researchers say that the facial wrappings were removed quite a while ago and revealed the features of a male baby with small ears, a sharp nose, and thin lips parted to show two teeth that are still white.

Radiologists performed a computed tomography (CT) scan, which provided three-dimensional images. A thorough analysis of the bones in the mummy's hand, the plates of his skull, and the roots of his teeth suggested that the child died at the age of 7 or 8 months. The scans also showed that his organs had been removed. This was part of the process of mummification. His brain had been extracted through the left nostril. In ancient Egypt, the viscera, or internal organs, of the dead were removed and dried, rinsed, bandaged, and then placed in Canopic jars or parcels, which were then placed with the body. These Canopic jars would be decorated with the images of the four sons of Horus: Hapy, Imseti, Duamutef, and Qebsenuf.

The most significant discovery from the scan was amulets — small charms — affixed everywhere to the wrappings encasing the body. According to Ikram, there were many amulets of high quality. That fact and the mummification technology show that this was an elite child who appeared to be well cared for and treasured.

Hildebolt snipped a thumbnail-size portion of the wrapping for carbon dating. Test results indicate that the infant lived between 30 B.C. and 130 A.D. According to this timeline, this child may have lived at the same time as Cleopatra and Mark Antony.

Hildebolt also extracted three DNA samples no bigger than the tip of a match. Geneticist Anne Bowcock analyzed the 2000-year-old DNA, still in surprisingly good condition, and determined that the infant's mother was European, possibly Greek or Roman. Bowcock then wanted to try to determine whether a genetic disease had befallen the boy. According to Wiman of the SLSC, DNA research is continuing; however, nothing conclusive has been found.

The infant mummy exhibit at the Science Center opened in May 2007 and will probably be on display through March 2008. It is being exhibited in conjunction with the movie, "Secrets of the Pharaohs," being shown in the Center's Omni Max theatre. The exhibit will be found just outside the Omni Max theatre, on the second floor. It features the infant mummy, enclosed in glass case, and a 7-1/2–minute video about the mummification process and the radiology and DNA testing performed on the mummy by Mallinckrodt Institute of Radiology and Washington University Medical Center.

Science Center staff members had worried that an exhibit would disrespect the dead. But, after consulting with Ikram, they concluded that the research and its presentation ultimately honor the baby's memory. The exhibit includes a prayer.

HISTORIC SITES

DEUTSCHHEIM STATE HISTORIC SITE

OPERATED BY THE MISSOURI DEPARTMENT
OF NATURAL RESOURCES
107-109 WEST SECOND STREET
TELEPHONE: 573-486-2200

The Deutschheim State Historic Site captures the culture and heritage of the Germans who immigrated to Missouri in the mid to late 19th century through exhibits and galleries of changing artifacts and photographs. These collections include home interiors, tools, implements, and garden plantings. The Pommer-Gentner and the Strehly Houses are the two primary buildings.

THE POMMER-GENTNER HOUSE

The Pommer-Gentner House and the Strehly House are part of the Deutschheim State Historic Site & Museum. The word *Deutschheim* combines the German words for "German" and "home." This term was used by early German writers to describe parts of Missouri from the 1820s through the 1850s, especially the area from St. Louis west to Boonville on the Missouri River and in Perry and Ste. Genevieve Counties south of St. Louis along the Mississippi River.

The Pommer-Gentner House was built in 1840 and is one of the oldest surviving buildings in Hermann. It is currently closed for restoration. When it reopens, it will feature furnishings that reflect the life of an aristocratic German family of the 1830s and 1840s. An example of high-style German *Klassizismus* (neoclassical) style, now rare in the Midwest, it was furnished with Chinese and German porcelains, German silver from 1810-1845, and Missouri-German and imported furniture.

Pommer-Gentner House

GASCONADE COUNTY HISTORICAL
SOCIETY ARCHIVES
AND RECORD CENTER

315 SCHILLER STREET
HERMANN, MO 65041
TELEPHONE: 573-486-4028

The records center is located in the former Farmers & Merchants Bank, built in 1909. Here one can read about Missouri history, the "War of the Rebellion" (what the German Society called the Civil War), Gasconade County history, Gasconade County families, and Missouri and Gasconade River history.

Volunteer staff is available to assist visitors who wish to use the records for researching the histories and genealogies of families in Gasconade County.

Files date from 1812 and include probate, circuit court, real estate, and county commission records. Also available are marriage, death, birth, and census records. Copies of the local newspaper are on microfilm. Also, the archive shop features books on local family history.

Gasconade County Historical Society

Inside the Gasconade County Historical Society

Records in the Gasconade County Historical Society

German School Museum
315 Schiller Street
Hermann, MO 65041
Telephone: 573-486-2017

The German School building at Fourth and Schiller streets is now a museum. It is maintained by a local organization, Historic Hermann, Inc., devoted to preserving Hermann's heritage. Built in 1871, the structure continued to serve as an elementary school until 1955. At that time, classes moved to the old high school on Washington Street, and the school building was deeded to Historic Hermann. To this cause, for 50 years, the community has donated items of interest that portray life in Hermann since its founding in 1836.

Currently, the museum's second floor includes the Heritage Room, the Children's Room, the River Room, and a Needlework Corner. On the main floor are the Schweighauser and Els Rooms. A third room is undergoing major renovations and will house additional exhibits and a gift shop.

The Clock Tower was added in 1890 and is considered a Hermann landmark. The clock must be wound at least once a week. Its working mechanisms can be viewed on the second floor of the museum.

Tours of the German School Museum are self-guided, but volunteers are on hand to answer questions. Several who attended the German School enjoy sharing stories about their school days with visitors.

The German School Museum is open from April through October. Hours are 10:00 a.m. to 4:00 p.m., Tuesday through Saturday, and noon to 4:00 p.m. on Sunday; it is closed on Monday. The museum is closed from November through March but is open when festivals are scheduled during those months. A nominal fee is charged for tours.

Groups are welcome to schedule special tours by calling the museum in advance.

Of course, remnants of the past still linger with the history of old buildings. Kate Gilmore, who used to work and clean at the German School Museum, told one story about some of those traces to us. Kate said that no matter what time of day or night she was cleaning in the school, especially in the clock tower, she could hear children running and playing in the schoolyard below. Of course, no one was there. She said she never felt scared working alone; she felt soothed and comforted by the children's "presence."

German School Musuem

Desk in the German School Museum

Desktop

OUR LADY OF SORROWS SHRINE
605 BLUFF STREET
RHINELAND, MO 65069
TELEPHONE: 573-236-4390

This area became a shrine in the early 1800s, when German settlers were having problems with their crops. There were torrential, unceasing rains, so the farmers made a pilgrimage to the shrine and prayed to the Virgin Mary under the dogwoods. Finally the rains stopped, and the farmers were able to get their crops out, according to Sylvia Bruckenhoff, parish member of Our Lady of Sorrows Catholic Church in Rhineland (so named because the land around Hermann reminded the Germans so much of their homeland).

There is an annual pilgrimage to the shrine in the spring. Bruckerhoff says that people have come to the shrine to pray for healing from lifelong infirmities and to seek healing from the injuries incurred in bad accidents. The shrine keeps holy water from the Grotto at

Entrance to the Our Lady of Sorrows Shrine

Shrine of Our Lady of Sorrows

HERMANN'S HAUNTS

Lourdes, France. Some of the pilgrims drink this water; others bathe in it. Bruckerhoff said that some have left crutches and other walking aids behind as they leave the shrine, healed.

One Sister Mary Hundeth came to the Shrine in 1940, suffering from a bronchial cyst. She visited the Shrine at Our Lady of Sorrows, prayed, and drank the water from Lourdes. She returned to her doctor to learn that the cysts had disappeared. "Many people have come to the Shrine since I have been at the parish, and we have seen many leave healed," said Bruckerhoff.

THE POOR FARM

These days, not many people remember the terms "poor house" or "poor farm." But these were real places in the first half of the 20th century, set up in many communities for the purpose of supporting the aged, the infirm, the disabled, and folks who were just down on their luck. The Poor Farm in Hermann, Missouri, was established in 1909 and lasted until 1954; it saw some through the Great Depression, long before Medicare or Medicaid.

James Kenker told us that Judge Randolph Puchta had lived on the Farm while he was growing up because his father was the supervisor, and his mother did the cooking for the residents. The elder Mr. Puchta had to make sure that the chores were done and that the residents were fed and bathed, Kinker related.

To keep the Poor Farm functioning smoothly, the able-bodied residents had to take care of the chores, according to accounts by locals. These included feeding livestock, cleaning up the place, and helping to cook for the elderly residents who were unable to do for themselves.

Residents grew and canned their own food and butchered their own livestock. The Poor House is now a private residence.

ROTUNDA IN THE CITY PARK

In 1876, The Gasconade County Agricultural Association purchased nearly 7 acres of land for the express purpose of having a site for agricultural and artistic exhibits. They hired artist Edward Robyn to design an exhibit hall. He created the Rotunda, a beautiful, gazebo-shaped building, which included support posts throughout the structure. These support beams, however, played havoc with the bystander's ability to view the displays and obstructed the view of the stage. Later, craftsman Johannes Bohlken devised a way for a central post to be built that would support the entire roof. This project was completed; but it is still apparent where the old posts were placed. The Brush & Pallet Club restored the Rotunda in 1951. Presently, the Club is looking to refurbish the Rotunda again and will gratefully accept any donations for the project to be completed. Donations may be sent to the Brush & Pallet Club, 123 Main, Hermann, MO 65041.

The Rotunda

Close-up of the door on the Rotunda

HERMANN'S HAUNTS

HERMANN CITY CEMETERY

Cemeteries can be fascinating places because they tell so much about the history of the residents, and perhaps are some haunted, as well. The Hermann City Cemetery is no different. According to Bruce Ketchum, Administrator of the Deutschheim State Historic Site, Hermann's history is fascinating because of the way the early residents thought. The Germans were Rationalists who had experienced social uprisings in their own country in 1848, although some had emigrated before this time. "They were very idealistic and seeking a highly individualistic and independent way of life when they came to America," said Ketchum. "So the people buried in this cemetery had endured many problems and hardships, and had worked hard to carve out their lives here."

Ketchum also said that a conch shell engraved on a tombstone is a sign of eternal life and a weeping willow is symbolic of sadness. Many of Hermann's honored dead are buried in this cemetery. These are just a few:

Hermann City Cemetery

- Laura Stark (née Feldmann) September/1854　September/1916

Married George Stark [was owner of Stone Hill]
- John Feldmann December/1825 – August/1899

Founder of Union of Freemen; was surgeon for the Union in the Civil War
- Teresa Feldmann 1822-1887

Was widowed when she married John Feldmann
- Eduard Muehl August/1800 – July/1854

"Honor the brave fighter for truth and human justice" Editor of the first and second newspapers in Hermann, MO
- Carl Strehly November/1810-September/1876

Typesetter for the first and second newspapers in Hermann, MO
- Sophia Strehly (née Schlinder)

Wife of Carl Strehly

Carl and Sophia's children:
- Rosa Strehly September/1865 - July/1962
- Carl Strehly November/1860 – December/1929
- G.H. Genter November/1814 – March/1888

One of the original 17 Hermannites
- Caroline Pommer

Owner of Pommer house; her husband (Buster) died before they could move from Philadelphia to Hermann

On the day that we investigated the cemetery, a sudden, strong wind at the top of the trees came out of nowhere and lasted about 10 minutes. Then the wind left as quickly as it had come.

On the windward side of the cemetery, next to where George Bayer is buried, is a grave with a tombstone engraved with a skull and crossbones. The skull and crossbones tombstone is so weathered that the text engraving is no longer legible, and so the grave is an enigma. No matter how hard we tried, we were unable to find out to whom this grave belonged. The young people in town said it belongs to a witch and that whoever touches the tombstone will be cursed. A town elder suggested the skull and crossbones to be a symbol once used by the Odd Fellows, and she produced an invitation with the same etching. Another story is that the tomb really has no one buried there at all—that the tombstone was used to mark where untold treasures

Tombstone with skull and crossbones

Close-up of skull and crossbones on tombstone

were buried. Still another story is that the skull and crossbones are an ancient symbol of Christianity.

The City Cemetery records are kept at the Gasconade Historical Society, but they are listed in books by family name. Because the name is not legible, the skull and crossbones marker cannot be traced by this means.

Who knows what secrets this marker is really hiding?

WINERIES

Bias Vineyards & Winery

P.O. Box 93
3166 Hwy B
Berger, MO 63014
Telephone: 573-834-5475
Toll free: 800-905-2427
www.biaswinery.com

This small, family-owned winery is 7 miles east of Hermann, in Berger, Missouri. It was started by Jim and Norma Bias in 1980 and has limited production.

The wines are produced with grapes from their own vineyards, not far from the winery itself. The farm and winery overlook the Missouri River Valley and sit high on the scenic bluffs. The proximity of the vineyard to the winery permits prompt crushing of the grapes when peak ripeness is achieved. In fact, all pressing, fermentation, aging, and bottling are performed on site, as well.

The Bias winery has an interesting history and a few spirits of its own. The only family member in the small family plot who has a marker is Charles Reinhardt, who was born September 1842 and died April 1891. The story goes that Mr. Reinhardt died while crossing Missouri Pacific railroad tracks, down the present day driveway and around the hill from the winery, as he was taking eggs to town to sell. It is ironic and sad that one of his small daughters also died at the same location, in the same manner, at a later date; she was about 2 or 3 years old at the time of death. The rest of the family's graves are marked with large, flat stones, with no names or dates indicating to whom they belong. There are 8 or 9 children, and 7 to 9 adults in this family plot.

Charles Reinhardt purchased the property in the late 1850s and built the large home. It had a basement/cellar, three large rooms on the first floor (a room was added later onto the back of the house where the original porch had been), and three large rooms on the second floor. The front of the house faced the Missouri river. In back, a few of the original outbuildings still stand. The larger of the two was a smokehouse; the smaller one, now leaning, was used as a woodshed originally, and perhaps as a chicken coop in later years.

Josephine was Charles' wife. It is said that she enjoyed smoking a corncob pipe but that when someone would come to call she would put the pipe away in the one of the pockets of her dress. Her dress caught fire several times because she had not snuffed out the fire sufficiently; however, it was not reported that she incurred any injuries from the occult pipe.

Josephine (Granny) outlived many of her children and was still living in the original house into the 1960s. In her later years, she lived in the room that was added onto the back that had been the porch area of the original house.

Carol and Kirk Grass and their employee Bonnie (Bonnie also worked for Jim and Norma Bias) say they feel and hear things inside the Bias winery. A picture of Norma Bias hung in the entryway for a year after her passing. The picture had been painted by one of the family. Norma's daughter wanted the picture but had loaned it to the new owners (Carol and Kirk) for a year. When the daughter came to fetch the picture, activity picked up in the winery. Carol and Bonnie both said they could feel Norma's presence. The sound of someone walking over the metal threshold can be heard when no one is there. The sound of doors opening and slamming can be heard, and no one but the employees, who are present and accounted for, is there.

Carol said they fell in love with the place when they originally bought it and that they love the peaceful feeling they get when they cross over the Union Pacific railroad tracks and head up the hill to the winery. They purchased the property with the intent to keep it, as much as possible, just the way it is. They also operate a microbrewery on the grounds named "Gruhlke's Microbrewery."

The Grasses grow five varieties of grapes: Seyval, Chambourcin, Vidal, DeChaunac, and Catawba.

BOMMARITO ESTATE ALMOND TREE WINERY
3718 GRANT SCHOOL ROAD
NEW HAVEN, MO 63068
TELEPHONE: 573-237-5158

The Bommarito Estate Almond Tree Winery is named after the almond tree that would not grow, according to Nick Bommarito, owner of the winery. Nick said that he had to go to great lengths to get the tree, which is not native to Missouri, to grow. He said he drilled holes to aerate the soil and put nitrogen sticks in the ground so the tree would bloom. To the astonishment of native Hermannites, the tree bloomed and produced a spectacular show of almond tree blossoms, a likeness of which graces the background of the labels for the Almond Tree wines.

Nick says to please come, bring your picnic basket, and enjoy a bottle of one of Missouri's most tasteful wines (to which the authors are most partial). Bommarito and his children founded this beautiful winery in 1996 in the rolling hills between Hermann and New Haven. Guests, 21 and older, may enjoy award-winning wines in a serene, park-like setting. Outdoor seating areas offer great views of summer sunsets and the vineyards. The tasting room has a fireplace for cool autumn days.

Vineyards at Bommarito Winery

Patio at Bommarito Winery

HERMANN'S HAUNTS

HERMANNHOF
WINERY

**330 EAST FIRST STREET
HERMANN, MO 65041
TELEPHONE: 800-393-0100
WWW.HERMANNHOF.COM**

Krepp's Brewery, established in 1852, later became the Hermannhof Winery. The cellars are unique in that they are built from brick and stone. The century-and-a-half-old building is registered as a National Historic Site.

Courtyard at Hermannhof Winery

Staff members say that Hugo, one of the brothers who operated the winery years ago, was killed in one of the cellars by a wine barrel that fell on top of him. According to Lisa Brandt, retail manager at the winery, his body was not discovered until 3 days later by one of the brothers. Staff members say the area in which this accident is supposed to have occurred still has a cold and eerie feeling about it, and they can feel Hugo's presence.

There is sycamore tree in the courtyard, the branches of which give the appearance of a hand with fingers extending upward. Staff member Billy Grace says that they believe this tree to be a portal to the netherworld and that they feel that souls pass through this portal regularly — especially those who have worked at the winery in the past. Depending on what season it is, the portal will be light (during less activity) and dark (during heightened activity).

Once, a photo was taken at the gate, coming in from the street; when it was developed, the wine masters saw what looked to be an "extra" standing by them.

Another time, a special tour was granted to a group of people who were allowed to go far into the cellars, an area not usually available to the public. Suddenly, all the lights went out, and the group was deep inside, helpless (without a flashlight), until the lights came on

Barrells in wine cellar at Hermannhof Winery

some 10 minutes later. A few participants had the "bejeebers" scared out of them.

Grace also said there is an area in the cellars known as the "Angel's Share," where two angels are carved on the wall. In days gone by, rational, scientific explanations for strange events were not always available. People had "spiritual" explanations for things they could not see or understand.

A share (or portion) of wine is lost because of aging and evaporation in oak barrels, particularly in American or French oak barrels. Because the scientific explanation of evaporation was not always understood, superstition often overtook reason as an explanation for the missing portion of wine. To prevent an evil connotation, the angel was placed on the wall to offer up the "missing" portion of the wine, which then became known as the "angel's share." The angel stood guard against an evil intruder.

Kropp's Brewery once served as a wine clearinghouse. The local residents and winemakers brought in their own wines to be blended. Locals say that the patrons never left with as much as they had when they arrived because they drank so much while they were at the winery. However, winemaking became secondary when the focus of the business became that of producing beer around the turn of the 20th century.

Prohibition forced the closing of the winery in 1920. The building was converted to apartments at the time and remained so until 1976, when Jim and Mary Dierberg purchased the building and started what is today the Hermanhoff Winery. They had purchased the Dierberg

Bank in Hermann and wanted to give something back to the community. Orville Heberle, winemaker, and Otto Klein, chemist, assisted the Dierbergs in their efforts.

Hermannhof's vineyards, planted by Julius Ruediger in 1837, are located above the confluence of the Missouri and Gasconade Rivers. Ruediger was a notable winemaker of his day; his vintner's stone and log cabin still stands in Hermannhof's Little Mountain Vineyard. A spring, located on the hill above the winery, provides constant water flow through the cellars, as well as constant humidity. This eliminates evaporation and helps to maintain the quality of the wine.

The flagship wine of Hermannhof is White Lady, a German-style white wine. Their sparkling wines are made in the classic French méthode *Champenoise*, and several wines are aged in oak casks made both in Missouri and in France. Hermannhof can boast an extensive list of award-winning wines.

OakGlenn Winery

1104 OakGlenn Place

Hermann, MO

Telephone: 573-486-5057

www.oakglenn.com

Tucked high away on the bluffs of the Missouri River, OakGlenn offers a breathtaking countryside view. It was once called "Schau-insland," or "look into the Country," because of its spectacular view. OakGlenn was established in 1859 by internationally known horticulturist and vintner, George Husmann. The George Husmann Wine Pavilion, open daily, offers a large selection of premium wines. There is live entertainment most Saturdays in the summer and fall.

Before Husmann became the vintner, his brother-in-law Carl Teubner owned the vineyard. Carl Teubner arrived on the Hermann scene in the fall of 1846. In February 1847, he purchased 200 acres immediately east of the village, including a high bluff on the Missouri River. He brought 8000 fruit trees and vines of the choicest varieties from Cincinnati, thereby introducing the attractive Herbemont grape to Missouri. Teubner's efforts formed what his eminent brother-in-law later described as the "nucleus of fruit growing and winemaking around Hermann," embodying the first reliable nursery in the state.

Oakglenn Winery Pavilion

Oktoberfest at Oakglenn Winery

Adam Puchta Winery

1947 Frene Creek Rd.
Hermann, MO 65041
Telephone: 573-486-5596
www.adampuchtawine.com

The California Gold Rush of 1849 inspired many people to head west to find their fortunes. Some, such as John Adam Puchta, succeeded. Adam founded the winery after returning home from the Gold Rush because he had indeed found enough gold to fund his own winery. He purchased a portion of his father's 600-acre farm and cleared the land for grape growing and farming. In 1855, he established the Adam Puchta & Son Wine Company.

Although the Gold Rush had been well under way by the time Adam and his brother Friedrick headed to California in 1852, they stayed for a couple of years and obtained the wealth that enabled them to return to Missouri to start the winery and Adam to marry Clementine Riefenstahl. The Reifenstahl family was among the first 17 settlers of the town of Hermann.

Adam and Clementine were successful with farming and winemaking until disaster struck in 1858 when Clementine died. A year later, Adam married Clementine's sister, Bertha Riefenstahl, who had been the first female child born in Hermann. Bertha and Adam had two children, Henry John and Clementine. However, the daughter died as a child, attesting to the hardships of the early years at the winery.

Adam continued to farm and make wine, but also found time to become a school director and road master. He, his wife, and family were members of the Evangelical Church.

After Adam's death in 1905, Henry John Puchta, Adam's son, continued the family operation of winemaking, along with his son Everett until 1919, when Prohibition closed the winery doors. The land has passed from generation to generation and the family has continued to farm it.

One of Everett's sons, Randolph, born in 1928, and Randolph's son Timothy, born in 1956, reopened Adam Puchta Winery in 1990. In 1994, Randolph and Eunice Puchta were recognized by the Missouri

Frene Creek at Adam Puchta Winery

Century Farm Club for their family's contributed to local, state, national, and international agriculture by owning and operating the same Missouri farm for 100 years or more.

The Adam Puchta Winery is once again producing world-class fine wines with the ambiance of old family tradition. In the past 3 years, their wines have had the distinction of earning 80 medals in state, national, and international competitions. In the year 2000, Puchta's 1997 Estate Bottled Norton received the Governor's Cup of Missouri, the state's highest honor. Adam Puchta Winery remains the oldest continuously owned family winery within the state and one of only a handful in the United States that date back to pre-Prohibition days.

PHOENIX WINERY
1840 HIGHWAY 50
(NEAR MT. STERLING – 25 MILES SW OF HERMANN)
SOUTH ON HWY 19 TO DRAKE
TELEPHONE: 573-437-6278
WWW.PHOENIXWINERY.COM

Guenther Heeb, owner, established the Phoenix Winery in 2000. He makes wine from nine French hybrid grape varietals that he grows on 10 acres. Heeb says that the building was erected in 1886 and was the rectory of a church that burned down in 1933.

With forebears born and raised near Germany's finest vineyards along the Rhine River, the Heeb family boasts a history that includes more than 200 years of family tradition in the making of premium wines. After taking a break from winemaking, Heeb has returned to doing what he loves best: creating fine wines for all to enjoy.

Heeb describes his vineyard and winery as a boutique, where he tries to maintain the German style of winemaking. The winery also has the Edelweiss Dining Club for private membership only.

ROBLLER VINEYARD
275 ROBLLER VINEYARD ROAD
NEW HAVEN, MO 63068
TELEPHONE: 573-237-3986
WWW.ROBLLERWINES.COM

Robller Vineyard is located in the picturesque countryside just east of New Haven, where rich, deep soils and gentle slopes provide excellent growing conditions and spectacular views. Families are always welcome — it's common to find a kite in the sky, dogs on the deck, and the winemaker pouring the day's samples. Pack up the kids and the picnic basket for a day to remember.

The original house was built in 1821 and is the oldest house in Franklin County.

The winery, established in 2000, is housed in a new building and is part of the Hermann Wine Trail. Robert and Lois Mueller are the owners.

Patio at Robller Vineyard

Vineyards at Robller Vineyard

STONE HILL WINERY
1110 STONE HILL HIGHWAY
HERMANN, MO 65041
TELEPHONE: 573-486-2221
WWW.STONEHILLWINERY.COM

When an establishment has remained many years, its history seems to have a way of embedding itself. The "psychic residue," or the etching of certain occurrences on the surrounding atmosphere, gives a place its ambiance. And such is the case with the wineries, where the passion of the fruit brings out the passion of its purveyors.

They say that "George," a long-past local inhabitant of Stone Hill Winery, is a good spirit, for the most part. He is always pulling pranks on the family. They suppose that George is the spirit of George Stark, who owned the winery from 1893 to the 1920s. George brought Stone Hill Winery to the enviable status of the world's third-largest winery, the second largest in the U.S. until Prohibition laid waste to his empire.

Stone Hill Winery

But some question whether he is a playful supernatural spirit or just a product of the imaginations of people who probably drank too much wine. Or is he a cover-up for things grown out of control? The mystery remains.

However, the Held family maintains that one of his manifestations was quite spectacular — or perhaps "spooktacular" for those more sensitive — when Stone Hill owner, Jim Held, purchased a three-piece chair set at an auction. He says he put the set in the attic in a very specific location — where he had room. When he returned to the attic to move it downstairs, the set had been moved to a completely different location in the attic, and no one seemed to know why because no one had been to the attic in the meantime.

Tom Held, Jim's son, said he always knew when George was around because he would find his sister Patty crawling out from under the piano bench in the living room. Patty said she had felt George's presence, and at times a fog or cloud could be seen that was rather weird, indeed. Also, they would hear George, mainly at night, and the house was never quiet. Tom said he was especially aware of this when he

Vintage Restaurant at Stone Hill

would have to climb three flights of stairs to close the windows in the tower when inclement weather was expected. "I was sure George was on my tail all the way up those flights and then back down," Tom said.

Occasionally a sudden loud crash from that area will resonate through the empty halls of the winery. Jim, realizing that he must check out the situation, thinks to himself that he is going to have to make a trip through the dark, wet caverns that lie beneath Stone Hill to discover the source of this terrible thud. He says he once made his way down the creaky, timeworn stairs, and on reaching the bottom he searched across the dimly lit room and looked directly into the stern eyes of George Stark — because his portrait hung with other formers owners along the wall. Jim then recognized the sound as the slamming of the heavy door of the walk-in cooler.

The strangest of all the family's experiences, however, occurred when Tom arrived in the museum area one day to find that the books stored in an old armoire were on the floor — that is to say, all of the books written in English were on the floor. Those written in German remained in the cabinet.

Stone Hill Bottles and Ribbons

WENWOOD FARM WINERY
1132 BRICK CHURCH ROAD
GASCONADE COUNTY, MO 65014
WWW.WENWOODFARMWINERY.COM

Wenwood Farm has indoor and outdoor seating, wine tasting, a gift shop, cheese and sausage baskets, and beautiful scenery.

Take Highway 19 south of Hermann and turn right on Highway 50. Go to Highway A and turn left at Mt. Sterling, and then left on Brick Church Road.

Wenwood owners Laura Neese and husband Tom Kalb live in the old farmhouse on the 400-acre farm. The rural setting for the winery is a former dairy farm that has converted the calf barn into a tasting room, the dairy barn into the wine production area, and the bull barn into the event pavilion.

Special events are a large part of the business. Redbud Fest in April, Heritage Fest in June, and Harvest Home Fest in September are three Winery events, as well as concerts during warm weather featuring musicians who play a wide variety of music including bluegrass, jazz, folk, blues, and even some Cajun. Winter events include a hayride, a Nouveau wine dinner and Christmas gatherings.

Swiss Meat Company sausages and cheeses are always available for sale, as are wine and soft drinks.

Wenwood Farm Winery

Harvest Home Festival at Wenwood

Deer at Wenwood Farm

TIN MILL BREWING CO.

FIRST AND GUTENBERG
HERMANN, MO 65041
TELEPHONE: 573-486-2275
WWW.TINMILLBREWING.COM
OWNERS DON & JEANNE GOSEN AND ELLEN DIERBERG SCHEPMAN

Tin Mill hosts a large brewery complex in downtown Hermann, housed in the former MFA Feed Store on Gutenberg. The owners make the majority of the brewery's German beers, which include a Light Pilsner, Full Bodied Lager, Dopplebock and Octoberfest beer. All of the raw materials for these beers are imported from Germany. "Our beers are all made in the traditional German brewing method using only lager yeast," said Gosen. "This gives the beer a dryer, more crisp flavor." There is a beer garden in the back of the building and also across the street from the brewery.

The Tin Mill Brewery is capable of producing more than 2000 barrels a year and will include a kegging and bottling line. The next phase of the brewery project will include the grain elevator on First Street next to the red caboose. The grain elevator will become a full-service restaurant and brewpub. "A separate brew system will be installed in this facility and will produce more of our seasonal and specialty beers," said Gosen. He said one example of this is an oatmeal stout that is aged in used Jack Daniels barrels for 6 months. The Tin Mill also makes a beer with ingredients grown on the new living history farm, under construction at the former Kallmeyer farm.

Tin Mill Brewing Company

Bar area at Tin Mill

BED
& BREAKFASTS

Town of Hermann

For adventurous travelers and explorers, the region in and around Hermann has more than 40 B & Bs. Each has its own history, ambiance, and type of hospitality. There is at least one that each traveler will find to his or her liking, and some have offered their own stories and history for this book.

Patty Kerr Gasthaus B&B and Massage

109 East 3rd Street
Hermann, MO 65041
Telephone: 573-486-2510
www.pattykerr.com
Todd and Nancy Satre, Innkeepers

Walk up the steps to the backyard and discover another world. The patio welcomes you with an umbrella table and hot tub, alongside the brick smokehouse, built in the 1890s. The garden is overflowing with sunflowers, hollyhocks, and other beautiful flowers. Butterflies and hummingbirds happily partake of the sweetness, as you will also. Choose from two great accommodations, The Iris Room or The Cottage. Both have queen-size beds, private baths, gas fireplaces, small refrigerators, coffee pots, microwaves, tables and chairs, movies, and air-conditioning. A full breakfast is delivered to your room in the morning! Book a massage with Nancy, a licensed massage therapist. Rates: $98-$108.

The house was built in two stages, circa 1840 and 1858-9. The earliest section of the house is half-timbered with brick nogging, probably dating to before 1841, and built by or for J.B. Idemann. At the time of the street grading, a local builder, John Quandt, Jr., acquired the property and added the east room, built of wood frame, and the brick first story beneath the original house, as well as a rear open porch. Sometime before 1892, the rear porch was framed in with new siding overall in either end wall of the house, and a brick wall was constructed at the rear elevation, second-story grade level. The brick smokehouse was built between1892 and 1898. Friedrick Kraemer, shoemaker, who probably had his shop on the ground floor, lived in the house for many years.

The doors and windows were replaced in 1991, and the originals were donated to the Daniel Boone Home in Defiance, Missouri. The

Patty Kerr Bed & Breakfast

Patty Kerr Bed & Breakfast

house was also sided at that time. The home and doors were featured in the December 1996 issue of *Country Home*. Still in view are the holes in the timbers where ropes once linked them together, a reminder their previous incarnation as a means of river transportation years ago.

WINE VALLEY INN

403 MARKET STREET
HERMANN, MO 65041
TELEPHONE: 573-486-0706
WWW.WINE-VALLEY-INN.COM
PAM AND RICHARD GILIG, INNKEEPERS

Pam Gilig and her husband Richard, owners of the Wine Valley Inn, say they hear the spirit of Mr. August Begamann often in the house, and he is quite a prankster, according to Pam. "Mr. B. built the two buildings with the same architecture, one for his son Lewis, and the other building a few blocks away for his son Armin," she said. The basement was for storage and supplies, the first floor was a mercantile, the residence was on the second floor, and the third floor was vacant.

Housekeeper Jeanie Schultz said that one day while she was folding laundry on the second floor she felt someone pinch her on the but-

Wine Valley Inn

tocks, and she was sure that her husband had come in without her knowledge. "I turned around and no one was there!" she exclaimed. "I feel Mr. Begemann's presence often, and we hear the elevator go from floor to floor randomly without anyone pressing the button to call for it. The elevator is haunted," she said. "It is programmed to stop and stay on the first floor unless it is called."

The proprietors have had some very funny and strange experiences at the B&B. They say they will find things moved about. Renovation for the bed and breakfast started in 2000, and during that time, Pam said she and her employees had things go missing. Towel racks that had been carefully counted out when purchased came up short when being installed. She said that many times things they had accounted for came up short. She said for a while she thought she was losing her mind, until she determined there must be something more to the disappearances than met the eye.

And there is a chandelier with five light bulbs in it, Gilig said. "All of which have been unscrewed. So of course, the lights won't come on," Schultz said. "I have to get on a chair and screw the light bulbs in so we can use the room."

Guest Room at Wine Valley Inn

Jeanie said she has seen what looks like a little girl walking down the hall on the second floor; also, a short man. Pam said she has seen a picture of Lewis Begemann, and he appears to have been a short man.

Pam said there is always more activity in the old building in the winter when it is quiet and not as many guests are present. She took us upstairs for a tour of the second floor. All felt a cold spot in the sitting area of room 203. Pam said she thought that this was in the area where the Begemanns lived. When we came downstairs, we told Jeanie of our experience. Jeanie said she always has to clean a spot on the floor in that area. Until she heard our story, she said she thought it was multiple messy guests that had spilled coffee in the same spot.

Pam also told us a story, as told to her by the Sanders sisters. The Sanders sisters had lived in the house as children and are now active octogenarians. They told Pam that they had lived on the second floor. They talked about the hats the ladies used to wear in those days, large ones with lots of frills. The sisters said they used to take dead pigeons and let them down on a string from their second floor balcony onto ladies' hats. They would clip the string and the ladies would walk away with more frills than they bargained for. They must have had the same prankster spirit as that left behind by Lewis Begemann, Pam related.

The bed and breakfast now houses a dining room on the first floor and eight units on the second floor. The Giligs have plans to make three loft apartments on the third floor and a wine and piano bar in the basement.

WOHLT HOUSE B & B

415 EAST FIRST STREET
HERMANN, MO 65041
TELEPHONE: 573-486-2394
WWW.WOHLTHOUSE.COM

Mr. August Wohlt, Hermann's first mayor, built the house four stories tall so he could see the boats being constructed on the shore of the Missouri River. That was his profession, shipbuilding. "The home was a mansion, for its time, "Jerry Watts said. He said that he and Gregersen, a guest at the B & B, often heard footsteps on the stairs. When they look to see who entered the B&B, no one is there. I stayed at this lodging and can attest to hearing someone walking about. When I opened the door to see who came in that night, no one was there.

Judy Gregersen said the strangest thing she has experienced happened one night as she removed her jewelry before going to sleep. "I left my necklace and earrings on the table beside the bed. In the morning I put on the necklace but could not find the earrings anywhere. I searched and searched and knew they had to be there. I moved the

Wohlt House Bed & Breakfast

Wohlt House Bed & Breakfast

phone and other things lying on the table, thinking I will surely see them,' she said.

Judy then went on about the business of the day and returned later in the afternoon, only to find the earrings in the place she had laid them, one perfectly on top of the other in the exact location where she had put them down.

Gregersen also stated that one day while she was in the attic she felt like someone was looking at her, and felt it to be Mr. Wohlt. She also said that one of her guests wrote the same story in the guest book.

According to Gregersen, her grandson at the age of about 3 years old was in the dining room one day and just looked into the corner and stared for the longest time and just stood silent and spellbound, and then this occurred again in the hallway at the first floor entrance. Gregersen said this child was always perceptive to the spiritual, or unseen side of life.

Gregersen noted that the home has an ambiance from another time and feels that Mr. Wohlt is happy with the renovations done since it was built in 1884. It is now on the National Register of Historic Places. "He seems to just watch over things, and never does anything spooky," she said.

August Wohlt was born in August 1853 and died in March 1927. He and his wife had no children but raised two nieces. One niece was to inherit the Wohlt house; the other niece was given a brick house that was built for her a few lots down the street.

Wohlt House Bed & Breakfast

HERMANN'S HAUNTS

B&Bs, Inns & Suites

in and around Hermann, Missouri

A SECRET VINE B&B

Telephone: 314-805-7946
www.secretvine.com

A STONY HILL GUEST HOUSE

Telephone: 573-237-4537
4344 Hwy E
New Haven, MO

APPRILL'S WINE VALLEY GETAWAY

Telephone: 573-486-3463
www.apprillw@aol.com

ALPENHORN GASTHAUS

Telephone: 573-486-8228
www.alpenhorngasthaus.com

BEAR VALLEY FARMERS MARKET B&B

Telephone: 573-252-4365
www.bearvalleyfarmers.com

CAMPBELL HOUSE B&B

Telephone: 573-486-1093
www.campbellhaus.com

CAPTAIN WOHLT INN

Telephone: 573-486-3357
www.captainwohltinn.com

CAT NAP INN

Telephone: 877-499-7446
www.acatnapinn.com

CARRIAGE HOUSE B&B LLC

Telephone: 573-486-0447
www.cadyfolkart.com

COUNTRY COTTAGE B&B

Telephone: 573-834-7602
www.countrycottagebb.com

DAYS INN BOONSLICK LODGE

Telephone: 573-835-7777
403 Boonslick Road
New Florence, MO

DREWAROSA

Telephone: 314-968-0906
www.drewarosa@peoplepc.com

EPPLE HAUS B&B

Telephone: 573-294-6203
www.epplebedandbreakfast.com

ESTHER'S AUSBLICK B&B

Telephone: 573-486-2170
236 West 2nd Street
Hermann, MO

EVIES GRAPEVINE SUITES

Telephone: 314-808-3756
103 East 4th Street
Hermann, MO

GRAPEVINE GUEST SUITE

Telephone: 573-486-5758
www.hermannguestsuites.com

GRAY STONE GUEST HOUSE

Telephone: 573-486-5758
www.hermannguestsuites.com

HARBOR HAUS INN & SUITES

Telephone: 573-486-2222
www.harborhausinn.com

HEALING STONE RETREAT & SPA

Telephone: 573-486-5000
www.healingstoneretreat.com

HERITAGE LODGING

Telephone: 573-486-3137
200 East 1st Street
Hermann, MO

HERMANN MOTEL

Telephone: 573-486-3131
112 East 10th Street
Hermann, MO

HERMANN HILL INN & COTTAGES

Telephone: 573-486-4455
www.hermannhill.com

HERMANN BLUFF GUEST HOUSE

Telephone: 573-486-2087
www.hermannbluff.com

IRON HORSE INN B&B

Telephone: 573-486-9152
www.theironhorseinn.net

LYDIA JOHNSON INN

Telephone: 573-486-0110
www.lydiajohnsoninn.com

LABOUBE FARMS

Telephone: 573-486-2222
www.laboubefarms.com

LES LAVANDES B&B

Telephone: 573-486-4774
www.leslavanderbandb.com

LOUTRE VALLEY FARM GUEST HOUSE

Telephone: 573-291-7865
352 Bader Road
Hermann, MO

MARKET STREET B&B

Telephone: 573-486-5597
210 Market Street
Hermann, MO

HERMANN'S HAUNTS

MEYER HILLTOP FARM B&B

Telephone: 573-486-5778
www.meyerhilltopfarm.com

MONTAGUES B&B

Telephone: 573-486-2035
www.mantaguesbedandbreakfast.com

MURPHY'S B&B

Telephone: 573-486-8847
www.murphysbedandbreakfast.com

NEUFELD-DAVIES B&B

Telephone: 573-486-8107
www.bedandbreakfast.com

PATTY KERR LLC B&B

Telephone: 573-486-2510
www.patttykerr.com

SECOND CREEK FARM B&B

Telephone: 573-437-6999
www.secondcreekfarm.com

SERENITY PLACE

Telephone: 573-486-0199
www.massageforyourhealth.com

SPIRIT HILL GUEST HOUSE

Telephone: 314-280-9943
www.spirithillinfo.com

SPIRIT IN THE SKY B&B

Telephone: 573-486-3569
2421 Catholic Church Road
Hermann, MO

STONE HAUS B&B

Telephone: 573-486-9169
www.stonehausbandb.com

THE DOLL HOUSE B&B

Telephone: 573-619-9623
www.thedollhousebandb.com

TWEENSTEEPLES B&B

Telephone: 573-486-0114
www.tweensteeples.com

HERMANN'S HAUNTS

WOHLT HOUSE B&B

Telephone: 573-486-2394
www.wohlthouse.com

WINE VALLEY INN

Telephone: 573-486-0706
www.wine-valley-inn.com

PHOTO CREDITS

Holly Drago and Jill Phillips 7, 8, 19, 47, 48, 50, 51, 59, 60, 61, 65

Courtesy of Missouri Department of Natural Resources 10, 11, 12, 13, 35

Courtesy of Missouri Historical Society St. Louis 17, 21, 22

Virginia Publishing, *Under Three Flags*, p. 3 (Osage Indians) and p. 14 (Daniel Boone)

Ken Kunstmann 36, 37

Marian Brickner 39, 40, 41, 42, 43, 45, 46, 55, 57, 58, 67, 68, 69, 77, 83, 84, 89, 90, 92, 94, 96, 98, 100, 102, 104

Carol Wamebold 62, 63

Courtesy of Wenwood Farm Winery 74, 75

Sandy Watts, The Wein Press 85, 86

Sonya Birk, Wine Valley Inn 85, 86, 87

Courtesy of Stone Hill Winery 70, 71, 72, 73, 81, 106